The Race to Place

Geoff Sims

Published by New Generation Publishing in 2019

Copyright © Geoff Sims 2019

The author asserts the moral right under the Copyright, Designs and Patents Act 1988 to be identified as the author of this work.

All Rights reserved. No part of this publication may be reproduced, stored in a retrieval system or transmitted, in any form or by any means without the prior consent of the author, nor be otherwise circulated in any form of binding or cover other than that which it is published and without a similar condition being imposed on the subsequent purchaser.

ISBN: 978-1-78955-621-6

www.newgeneration-publishing.com

New Generation Publishing

Contents

About the author	v
Introduction	vii
1 The Business Development or Sales Call	1
The gatekeepers	4
Opening the dialogue	9
2 The Client Visit	12
1. Open	13
2. Question	14
3. Listen	20
4. Clarify	23
5. Sell	26
6. Handle objections	29
7. Close	30
3 Handling Objections	32
Understanding objections	32
Avoid conflict	34
Types of objection	34
Viewing objections as a buying signal	44
4 The Candidate Interview	46
The seven steps	48
5 Conclusion	53
The "magic circle" of recruitment	53
A final message	54

About the author

Geoff began his professional career as an accountant with Unilever, Litton Industries and the Hunting Group. He moved into recruitment, joining the Hays team in Leeds as a trainee consultant in 1984. Over the next 20 years he was promoted to a series of directorships within Hays in accountancy and finance, and in the Office Support and contact centres.

Since then, Geoff has been instrumental in the development of Hays businesses across the UK. Today, Hays is a leading international supplier of permanent and interim staff. In 2011 he was appointed managing director for all the Hays businesses in the West and Wales region, then moved to his last role in the company, as well as continuing his national leadership of Hays Office Support. He also established the Hays business in Sweden, and was actively involved in early ventures in the Netherlands that led to the acquisition and growth of the business there.

Geoff spent many years as a judge of the European Call Centre and Customer Service Awards, and sat on the council for the Confederation of British Industry (CBI) in the East of England. He appears regularly on *BBC East* as a commentator on local employment trends and issues. He is also proud to be part of Leeds University Business School Management division's Leaders in Residence Programme.

With more than 30 years experience in the recruitment industry, Geoff ended his corporate career as Hays managing director in the East of England and now runs his own recruitment consultancy business: Waq'e Consultants (http://waqeconsulting.co.uk)

Introduction

The aim of this book is to help individuals working in recruitment, or embarking on their career in a recruitment agency.

When I started in recruitment more than 30 years ago, life was very different – no internet, mobile phones, customer relationship management or candidate databases, and very little compliance by way of legislation regarding verification of candidate eligibility. Most of this technology and process makes life easier for the consultant today, but the combination makes focusing on outcomes more of a challenge. The key measures back then were the number of interviews you arranged with your clients each week, or the number of temporary worker starters you had each week. That was the only information your manager was interested in, and the only data you could easily provide.

Today, a recruitment consultant is measured on every part of their role. If you focus on achieving the outcomes as a priority, your other performance measures will take care of themselves. So embrace change, judge yourself on what you do today rather than what you did yesterday, take responsibility for your actions and you will succeed.

If there is one message that I would like anyone reading this book to take away, it is that the fundamentals of recruitment consultancy have not changed, but everything else has. This book covers the basic sales activities, tips and techniques that form the backbone of a successful career in this sector.

1
The Business Development or Sales Call

The most important aspect of successful sales calling is focusing on the desired outcome. This should not be overcomplicated. It is also important not to confuse an excuse for calling with the overall objective. It is best to keep objectives simple:

1. register a new vacancy
2. arrange a face-to-face meeting
3. leave a "foot in the door" (FITD)

These objectives must be SMART:

Specific
Measurable
Aspirational
Realistic
Time dependent

– which applies to everything the consultant attempts. In the context of the recruitment sales call, the "T" (timescale) is the duration of the call. Many textbooks use "Achievable" for the "A" in SMART goals, but my logic is that if it is aspirational yet also realistic, it is naturally achievable, so why not aim high?

I often ask the question of consultants I am training what they believe their objectives to be. They can reply with anything from "building rapport" to "selling the company" and "obtaining information" – none of which are SMART goals, using the above definition. Other responses can include "marketing an event or seminar", "taking a reference" or "aftercare". All of these are good *excuses* for making a client call; however, if they are the *objective*, there is a danger that the call will be completed without asking for an opportunity to recruit for the company, because the focus is on the wrong outcome.

For example, a call to invite a potential client to an event is turned into a sales call by simply asking: "What can I help you with at the moment?" before ending the call. Without this question the consultant is wasting an opportunity. Many times I have watched a consultant celebrate a successful call because the target has agreed to attend an event, only to find that when they meet the individual, they learn that at the time the call was made, the target was recruiting – an opportunity lost.

Having identified our primary objective – seeking an opportunity to recruit – we need to understand our fall-back position (FITD). If there appears to be no opportunity to support the client, and no chance of arranging a face-to-face meeting, the last resort is to gain some commitment from the call that is within our control. Some calls may feel like a win if they end with an agreement for a future opportunity to recruit, or to receive further information about something. Many believe that agreeing a promise of an opportunity to recruit next time, or to simply receive information, satisfies this objective. I disagree, as it relinquishes control to the prospect rather than the sales caller.

Instead, a successful call should end with the consultant thanking the potential client for their time, and suggesting that they will call again in a few weeks. The most common response that this will get is "Yes, fine" or "OK" – not because there is an actual agreement, but because the potential client wants the call to end. Here, it is imperative that the time and date are kept tentative, because a call-back appointment suggests that the subsequent call will definitely take place, which is likely to lead to some debate about its relevance. The potential client's instinctive reply of "Yes, fine" or "OK" is uttered without anxiety that there will definitely be follow-up discussion. However, the potential client has unwittingly agreed to a follow-up call, which can be used later to the consultant's advantage.

When following up in a few weeks, the consultant should say at the start of the call: "I am sure you remember we spoke a few weeks ago, and we agreed to have a further conversation." First, the opening "I am sure you remember" will trigger either conscious or subconscious thought in the client trying to recall the conversation, and the power of "we agreed" encourages the client into offering more respect to the caller. This must be followed by a credible open question to start the conversation (see "Opening the Dialogue" below). Obviously, this may not ensure a successful outcome, but will help to create an environment for a more productive dialogue.

The gatekeepers

The first hurdle to overcome when calling any potential client is the gatekeeper. This generally manifests in four ways:

1. The receptionist
2. The PA
3. The colleague
4. The message system, or voicemail

Let's look at these in turn.

The receptionist

Most consultants I have trained over the years believe that the client's receptionist is the toughest to overcome. Having spent more than 30 years in recruitment, I have never seen a job specification that suggests that this individual is expected to screen calls – in fact, taken literally, it suggests quite the reverse!

So why do the majority of sales callers in recruitment believe this to be the case? Generally you will find that the answer to this lies with the caller, and how and what they say when asking to speak to the individual they wish to target. By being too polite, for example, "Please could you put me through to …" a message is being sent to the receptionist's subconscious, giving them full authority to decide whether to put you through or not, without realising it – creating a gatekeeper that did not exist before.

To make sure that the chances of being connected to the target are improved, try the following method. It is essential to know the potential client's name beforehand, as you need to send a psychological message that you are expecting to be put through.

Let's assume I am the target client. The technique would be:

Consultant: Good morning/good afternoon, Geoff Sims please.
Receptionist: Who is calling?
Consultant: Jane Smith.

At this stage it is important that no company name is given, and that it is delivered in an assertive tone, as if it is a name that should be known. The chance of more questions coming back diminishes at each stage; however if there is a subsequent response, it is likely to be:

Receptionist: And is there a company name?
Consultant: Yes, [your company name].

State this in the same tone and with the same assertiveness as before. Over the years I have found that many trainees struggle with this, as their self-perception of sounding assertive is misguided, or they tend to say too much, lessening their chances of being put through to the target.

Here, it's important to understand that there is a fine balance between assertiveness and aggression which must not be crossed. Most callers think that the latter helps them achieve the former – which should not be the case!

The PA

The job specification of a modern-day PA is wholeheartedly to be a gatekeeper. Their goal is to make the life of their boss – or more frequently, bosses – easier and more organised. PAs are highly capable individuals who have chosen their role in the company, and are proud of it. One of my previous employers surveyed more than 2,000 PAs in the UK, asking, among many questions, the following:

1. "Do you believe you could do your boss's job?"
2. "Would you like to do your boss's job?"

More than 90 per cent of those answering this question said that they felt they could perform the role, yet only 10 per cent would want to do so.

Treating these individuals with the respect

they deserve is the key to success, so discuss features and benefits as you would with any other important client. Many PAs are recruiters themselves, and most will have an input into the decisions made by their boss. If there is no way that you are going to be able to talk to the boss, having tried the technique above, then the next advice is to call at a time when the PA is not there.

The colleague

You may strike lucky and get directly through to your target; however, you are more likely to get through to a colleague. If you do, begin the conversation by using your assertive "receptionist" technique. If the person taking the call is junior to the target, and they perceive you by your tone to be important, they will be more concerned with putting you through efficiently than screening your call. Your instinct will quickly tell you if this is the case or not, and if not – that is, if the person is as senior or more senior to your target – move quickly into "PA respect" mode.

The message system, or voicemail

Finally, do we leave a message on automated

voicemail or not? Many have opposing views on this question, and it does depend on your relationship with the potential client to a large degree. There is no point in leaving any message unless you are including a reason for the person to call back, known as a "hook". The message you leave should be concise and to the point, and there must be a perceived benefit, otherwise the call will not be returned.

A strong candidate based on your knowledge of the company, individual or market sector would be such a reason. An event seminar or salary survey could be a similar benefit. Ego is another driver for someone to return a call – don't forget, you are calling from a recruitment company and the person might perceive you as headhunting *them*, provided that you don't leave too long a message.

Opening the dialogue

So we have negotiated past the gatekeeper and reached the most important part of the sales call: the opening. Textbooks disagree as to how long you have a target's attention for, but I always work on the basis of about 20 seconds. In that time we have to achieve the following:

- Introduce ourselves
- State the reason for the call
- Highlight the benefit linked to the reason
- Ask an open question
- Listen and wait for a response

The above is relatively self-explanatory, but the hardest aspect is often the benefit linked to the reason for calling – as mentioned previously, consultants are not always the best at translating features into benefits. It is also important that the consultant is not afraid of silence on the call: many do not wait for the answer to their question, and ask a subsequent question to fill the gap.

Sales calls made by recruitment consultants should not be scripted, as it can create a false discussion and dilute your ability to listen. Having said that, preparing and writing down an opening can help to ensure a more productive call. The call should proceed by encouraging a dialogue: ask open and probing questions to acquire information, and closed questions to attempt your objective. If this does not achieve the goal, revert to open questions on a different topic. Again, textbooks disagree on how many times to revert back to open questions – in fact, research points towards doing this five times before the call enters the territory where 65 per cent of objectives are achieved.

You will instinctively have a view of when you need to end the call, but this is based on your own perception of what you would be happy with, if you were the client. My advice is, when you feel this discomfort, try one more time! (The objections that have to be overcome during this stage, and the techniques to use, are discussed in more detail in Chapter 3.)

2
The Client Visit

This chapter covers the physical meeting with a potential client. (This interaction follows a cycle which will be discussed further in Chapter 5.)

The seven-step cycle is as follows:

1. Open
2. Question
3. Listen
4. Clarify
5. Sell
6. Handle objections
7. Close

This cycle can be applied to any interaction, albeit tailored accordingly to a short, sharp telephone sales call (covered in Chapter 1), or a more formal face-to-face sales meeting. It even applies to a lengthy tender or bid process, although obviously the timescales between stages will be extended.

If we dissect the list above, we can see how this works in practice. The opening introduction, or "making the contract", is discussed in detail in the client meeting (and was covered in the first 20 seconds of the telephone call).

1. Open
Making the contract

The introduction or "making your contract" is the scene-setter for the conversation to follow. Most recipients of this sales process are instinctively suspicious of the motives of the person approaching them. Unfortunately, the world of recruitment is littered with poorly trained and incompetent sales professionals who do not establish the needs of the client properly in order to create a "win-win" situation. To do this, it is important to explain the path that the discussion will follow, so that both parties understand the journey and the subsequent benefit to them.

We call this part of the process "making your contract" because that is exactly what it is. Let's assume you have secured a meeting with a potential client whom you have not met before. No doubt you don't need to be told that prior to the meeting you will have researched the company and, where possible, the individual you will be seeing. However, it is important that you don't make any assumptions or form any judgements from this preparatory work.

On arrival at the company, you will be asked to wait for the client in reception. Your contact or their representative arrives and after a handshake – firm, naturally! – you are escorted to the room where the meeting will be conducted.

One mistake many make during this period is to start selling in the lift or on the stairs. There are many reasons why this is inappropriate – not least the fact that no rapport has been built with the potential client at this stage. However, it is likely that some conversation will be necessary at this point, so a compliment on the office or surroundings can work well. If you feel that such a comment would be inappropriate based on the environment, you can always resort to a general topic such as the weather. On most occasions, if you keep quiet, the person you are meeting will break the ice and lead the conversation for you.

2. Question
Establishing a connection
You are now seated in the meeting room and ready to start the process. The first thing is to

pass your business card to your potential client. This action is a credible way to start the meeting formally, and it gives them peace of mind that they won't forget your name. Over the years, I have seen many such individuals glance at my card before addressing me.

Begin with the contract: start by thanking the individual for their time and the opportunity to meet with them. Then, explain that you would like to learn as much as possible about their company, which will enable you to identify features of your service which will benefit them the most: that is, "help me help you". Some companies train their consultants to hand over an agenda at this point, but this is not a technique I have employed. I am not saying don't use an agenda at all – it can be a useful tool when you are inexperienced in controlling a meeting, and more visually-oriented clients benefit from it – just that this can make the interaction too formal, and the contract between two parties is personal.

So to be clear, the contract is: give me an overview of your company and requirements, and in return I will explain how I can benefit you – "win-win".

Dealing with initial objections

On occasions a potential client might ambush you at this point with an early objection to handle, and will not let you take control of the conversation, as discussed previously. Here, the mistake many consultants make is to press on regardless, which is futile because the other person will not hear anything until they have aired their grievance or issue.

In this situation, overcome their objection using the techniques discussed in Chapter 3, and then re-engage with making your contract – in essence, clear the air first. In these early stages of discussion with your potential client, you will be naturally relying on your instincts to position the tone of the meeting. Sometimes you might be meeting in your contact's office, which is also useful, as it can give you valuable insight into the person in front of you. Whether you are gathering data by instinct or observation, make sure you do not assume anything; instead, use the information to prompt a question either to confirm your assumptions or employ an appropriate mode of address.

Case Study: Handling a difficult client

Discussing this situation reminds me of the first meeting I had with an individual who became one of my biggest and most loyal clients. As a company we had an outsourcing contract with a major technology firm, which was a very successful and lucrative partnership. However, there was one part of the relationship that was not going quite so well. There are many specialist ways of recruiting in niche areas, but there were none more so than the world of contact centres in the late 1990s to early 2000s.

This scenario involves an individual who was responsible for this entire sector from a recruitment perspective. As a company, we had not exactly covered ourselves in glory thus far, and as managing director of a specialist division in this area, I went to meet the client to try and rectify the situation.

I was anticipating the meeting with some trepidation as the client had a reputation for having an aggressive and direct approach. I was ushered into his office and sat down – as I did so, I noticed a framed emblem of (luckily) my favourite football team. My instincts told me that I should revisit my sighting later, rather than mention it there and then.

I then attempted to make my contract – an attempt which failed miserably! The client launched at me verbally – most of which, frankly, was hot air – but the gist was that he did not believe my company was capable of giving him what he wanted, as we were not experts in his field. He had a valid point, as we had not used any of my experts in this sector on the project thus far, and he had been let down.

I listened to his concerns, making sure I noted down any specific issues so I could refer back to them a little later, when it was my turn to speak. First, it was really important to get everything out in the open, so that all the issues could be addressed; and second, so that he felt he was being listened to (something of huge importance to this particular individual, as I was to learn over time!).

I dutifully listened to his offload, during which I kept prodding for more issues – in such a situation it is important to uncover every problem. The first thing I did was to apologise sincerely that he felt the way he did, before addressing each point in turn. Words are as important as tone: do not use words that accept the service was poor unless you have no alternative, but do apologise for the way that the person feels about the situation or the issue in hand. I then revisited each point in turn and discussed possible solutions for each one, giving anecdotes of how similar challenges had been resolved with other companies, in order to gain credibility.

Having established a rapport, I then referred back to the football team emblem. This proved to be a real icebreaker, and we spent the next 20 minutes or so sharing the highs and lows of supporting our beloved team. That was the start of a mutually beneficial, long-term relationship.

> My team excelled in their subsequent delivery, and throughout the remainder of the individual's career across five different companies, I was always his first call for recruitment.

3. Listen
The importance of questioning and listening

The next part of the interaction is the questioning and listening stage. Individuals generally enjoy talking about the company that they represent, and we should demonstrate patience even when their conversation is not relevant: allow them to talk.

Conversely, not all people you meet will be as verbose, and you must demonstrate good questioning and active listening skills. Many salespeople I have worked with over the years cannot resist jumping in when they hear something which presents an opportunity for them to gain. Whatever you do, don't fall into this trap; just note the information down and highlight it with an asterisk or similar, so that you can return to it later in the discussion. The questions you ask here should be open, simply anything that cannot be answered with a flat "yes" or "no".

Typically, these questions start with:

- what
- why
- how
- when
- where
- describe
- explain, etc.

I advise many trainees to write a list of open questions that they are comfortable to use, and tell them commit these to memory, so they can apply them when needed. Control of any discussion is through questioning and listening, rather than talking.

Active listening

Active listening is important, as is any body language which shows interest in the discussion. Nodding, smiling, leaning forward and making notes are all good examples of active listening. It is important to make sure you have all the information required to establish the best solution for your potential client. If you do not feel that you have sufficient detail on any area, use probing questions to get a fuller understanding.

A probing question is usually an open question, and provides an excellent way of demonstrating interest in the subject. Occasionally, you can use a closed question to probe when you are confirming your understanding of the information given, for example: "So would I be correct in thinking you have a need for this service?" The answer has to be "yes" or "no" – invaluable information to you as confirmation of potential need. This part of the interaction is where you have to demonstrate patience and understanding: only move to the next stage when you have all of the information you need, and make no attempt to sell anything this early in the meeting.

In order to create your best opportunity to achieve your sales objective, you must fully understand your own product and the benefits it offers for the client. Different users of your service or product will desire different benefits, and it becomes your responsibility to explain the links between what you offer and how it can help them achieve their goals. Not all the service features or products that you offer will be relevant to the potential client. For example, a family of four would have no use for a two-seater sports car as their family car; however, assuming that a family would only look to buy a four-seater is also wrong, as it might be a second car purchase.

So, in this stage you have listened intently to the client describe their company, and then through questioning, guided the individual to provide the information that you require.

4. Clarify
Check your understanding

It is now the time to clarify your understanding of the potential challenges that the client faces. In some situations you might not have been able to extract the information you require. The first way to clarity is to simply explain your understanding of the discussions so far, and ask them to confirm or otherwise.

On some occasions you may still not be satisfied that you fully understand: what you can do in such a situation is to give an anecdote of working with a similar organisation to your potential client's, describing the challenges that it faced. The topic is not selected at random, but on the basis of your summation thus far. To demonstrate the point, you might have to focus on an area in which the client does not expect you to be able to help.

> ## Case study:
> ## How anecdotes can help
>
> Here I refer back to my years in contact centre recruitment. The strategy I defined for my company's entry into the market was that we would try and support our clients with recruitment, onboarding and retention of staff. My rationale was that the more we became a partner to the client, the more trust – and therefore opportunity – would manifest.
>
> The target clients – large contact centres with constant recruitment or new set-ups – were not used to a recruitment company wanting to improve their retention, so it was very unusual for a client to discuss their staffing attrition instead of purely focusing on the number of new hires that they required each month.
>
> I would always ask but sometimes received a frosty response – often where

there was a problem. So I would talk about other centres and their challenges with retaining staff. This achieved two things: first, it demonstrated my expertise, which gained credibility; and second, it gave peace of mind to the client that their challenges were not unique, encouraging them to open up without embarrassment.

The main point here is the importance of questioning, listening and clarifying your understanding. These are all important facets of the interaction, but questioning and listening stand out as the most crucial. As mentioned previously, you can control any interaction through the ability to question and listen; however, up to and including this stage of the journey, the person you are engaging with is the most important element, and they must be made to feel that way. A high proportion of salespeople are driven by ego – in fact, it is almost a prerequisite to enable them to deal with rejection – but a good consultant will need to hide their ego in order to obtain the information required at this stage.

5. Sell

Translating client needs into benefits and services

Before moving forward, we should have a strong understanding of the requirements of our potential client and the challenges they face. It is now our time to be a translator or interpreter on their behalf. Why this description? Because it is our responsibility to identify the features of our product or service that are relevant, and translate them into benefits that relate to them. The more familiar a salesperson is with what they are selling, the less likely they are to convert features into benefits for the client.

I am not sure whether consultants become blasé or lazy, or perhaps a little of both. I prefer to believe that it stems from a familiarity with a product or service that we automatically assume everyone else understands. To give an example of this laziness in recruitment, the consultant might be selling an "experienced, immediately available candidate". The fact that the candidate is immediately available is a feature of that individual. The benefit of their experience is less training required and a quicker speed to competency, saving the client time and money, and giving them peace of mind. The benefit of immediate availability is not always as obvious to the client as it is to the consultant. They need to be told.

Engage the client
Having assimilated all the information you require, now is the time to start to engage the client with how you can help them. Inexperienced recruitment consultants often make the mistake of reeling off everything that their company offers, leaving the client to sort the wheat from the chaff.

My recruitment career was with a global recruiter operating in numerous countries around the world, and I have witnessed many inexperienced consultants telling a small, privately owned business how big we were and how many countries we operated in globally. While this is happening you can see the client switch off, perceiving that they will be unable to afford to use us, or that the candidates supplied will be unsuitable for their requirements. In that situation, the message should have been more about a local office network that supports companies of all types and size.

Case study: Understanding client culture

It is important to understand the culture of the market in which you operate. A good example of this was when I set up a recruitment operation in Sweden. The UK market was mature compared to the Scandinavian market, and at the time had a very different business culture, not to mention employment laws.

The first two or three months of operating were slow, and I decided to accelerate our development. In the UK, one way of achieving this is forwarding profiles of available candidates to potential employers. I spoke to a number of finance and information technology candidates, and obtained their permission to market them proactively. The mailing was all prepared and duly dispatched to more than 500 Stockholm employers, hoping for a positive response.

This activity had a huge impact but not necessarily as planned, as it created uproar, suggesting that my action was

> morally questionable and unprofessional. The issue was that the recruitment sector in Sweden worked in a different way at the time: candidates were sourced exclusively after the consultant had been retained by the recruiting organisation. The next week was spent dealing with these outraged potential clients; however, the skill of my team locally did manage to convert this into some strong client relationships.

Make the pitch
It is now time to make your pitch to the client. During the information-gathering stage you will have noted the key challenges faced by your potential client and their organisation. So, proceed by addressing each point in turn, explaining how you can help by linking each challenge to the relevant feature of your service that will provide the solution.

6. Handle objections
The next stage is to handle any objections that they will raise (this is covered in detail in Chapter 3).

7. Close

Having overcome the client's objections, it is important to close by gaining some measurable actions or outcomes, as without this the meeting has been a waste of time.

What is a measurable action? The answer is an agreed outcome between the client and the consultant that involves an action from both parties. If you can visualise a set of steps towards a goal that you want to achieve, the goal in recruitment at the top of these steps is to have a loyal client with whom you build a long-term relationship, and recruit for whenever they have a vacancy to fill.

In the very first engagement with the client, we are standing at the bottom of the steps, aiming to get to the top. Every time we interact with a client, we should be ensuring that we have climbed at least one step. From the very fact that we have arranged to meet the client, we have climbed halfway up. If the client has current recruitment requirements, the obvious answer to the question posed is an agreement that you will be able to recommend suitable candidates, with a diarised follow-up discussion to review your submission – a measurable step forward.

In the same scenario, you could advance at

least two steps forward by agreeing with the client how many interviews they would want to undertake and in what timeframe, and agreeing that they will give you total exclusivity to select candidates and arrange interviews for them.

However, it is more likely that the client you have visited has no current recruitment requirements. In this scenario, it is harder to define a measurable outcome from the client meeting. The secret in this situation is to make sure that you have a diarised agreement for a future discussion to continue to build the relationship. In this instance, a specific date is important because if the client is reticent to agree, it is likely to be a sign that you have not fully unearthed or sufficiently handled their objections. Therefore, it is important that you understand why this is the case – this will give you a further opportunity to overcome any residual objections, and allow you to move forward.

3
Handling Objections

Understanding objections

As mentioned in Chapter 2, the main reason that recruitment consultants fail to achieve their sales goals is that they do not overcome, or in some cases even unearth, client objections. The *Oxford English Dictionary* definition of objection is "An expression or feeling of disapproval or opposition; a reason for disagreeing." This would suggest that objection is a hurdle to overcome, which is how most consultants view it. However, viewing objection in this way creates the wrong mindset, and has a negative impact on the approach taken. The key point to remember is that people will always have questions or need clarifications around any purchase they make, so without objections there will be no sale. As a result, I encourage consultants to welcome objections and treat them as buying signals: they are a sign that the client is listening and showing interest, rather than putting barriers in the way of progress.

Another key point to remember is that the first objection a client gives is very rarely the real one, and so it is important that the consultant does not try and handle the objection until they understand the full scenario. It is also essential that nothing is assumed, which is another trap into which many consultants fall. A good example of this is when consultants are faced with the objection, "Your service is too expensive." The correct response would be something along the lines of: "What are you comparing us to?"

Many consultants assume that the comparison is to other competing agencies, and start negotiating on price. It may be that this is the case, but equally, those comparisons could be to an in-house recruitment team, staff bank or even a contracted relationship with a competitor – which is a different objection altogether.

Example

I tend to liken handling objections to tracing your family tree. For example, if you were trying to trace your way up the tree, from yourself to great-grandfather Billy, and you made the wrong assumption at any stage by not confirming the facts, you would end up in the wrong branch of the family.

The only way to correct the mistake is to retrace your steps and start again. It is unlikely that you will have sufficient time to do this with a client, so it is important not to assume, but to get it right first time.

Avoid conflict

It is also necessary to take any possible conflict out of the situation. This encourages the potential client to share more information without feeling threatened. My own way of diffusing these types of situations is to say "That's interesting", before asking the relevant questions to gain the information required. As with any communication the time has to be right, and it is important not to sound aggressive or condescending.

Types of objection

Some of the most frequent objections that consultants face are:

- Too expensive
- The company is loyal to a competitor

- There is an established preferred supplier list
- Not allowed due to company policy
- The company has its own recruitment team
- The decision-maker or organisation has had a bad experience with an agency
- There are no current recruitment requirements
- Lack of understanding of the range of services available

As mentioned previously, it is important to understand what the real objection is before progressing with the conversation. We also know that the first objection stated is not necessarily the real one. For example:

Client: It's our company policy not to use agencies.
Consultant: Oh, that's interesting. Why is that?
Client: Because you're too expensive.
Consultant: So, what are you comparing us to?
Client: Our own recruitment team.
Consultant: Why does your company follow that path?
Client: Because our head of recruitment had a bad experience.

In this example, although the first response was "company policy" and the second "too expensive", the comparison to make is with "their own recruitment team" in the same scenario after the first pushback, namely "company policy". Here, the actual reason for objection is "Because our head of recruitment had a bad experience" – which requires a very different approach to overcome.

This highlights that the real objection to overcome is only established through patience and questioning. There are other options to each stage, and this could materialise as "too expensive" compared to "our chosen agency", so competitor loyalty becomes the real objection to overcome. If the real objection is in the "most frequent" list outlined above, the method to overcome them would be as follows.

Too expensive

Identify in detail what the potential client's current method of recruitment is, and the detail of the service that would need to be provided. Compare and analyse the component parts of that process with what you can provide, before highlighting the extra benefits over and above this.

Company is loyal to a competitor

Your initial response should be "That is good to hear, because it is the type of relationship we enjoy with our key clients." This helps to diffuse potential conflict. The follow-up question should be: "What is it you like about the service you get from them?" Using this particular question eradicates the risk of confrontation; it also makes it easier for the potential client to talk about what they like, rather than what they don't – especially if they have been involved in the original decision to appoint.

It is essential to keep probing, making a list of all that the client likes about the service: it is a reasonable assumption that their omissions are what they don't like. However, even the "likes" can create an opportunity, when related to the services you offer.

Example

I once spoke to a potential client who stated that one of the things that they liked about their chosen recruitment company was that CVs were sent to them within 48 hours. This was duly noted and highlighted, but then the conversation progressed until all the likes had been listed, before returning to the individual items.

In relation to the CVs within 48 hours point, the follow-up question was: "How important is it to you to receive CVs quickly after registering a position?" The client replied, "Paramount." The company I represented prided itself in providing CVs the same day to all of our clients, so even a perceived strength in our competitor by the client transpired to be an opportunity to make a positive comparison over time.

Established preferred supplier list

When facing a preferred supplier list that you are not on, it is simply a case of trying to establish how you can get your company on it. Ask questions that indicate when it is up for renewal, who owns it, and any other relevant information. It is common for both parties not to actually understand who is on the client's list, so again it is sensible not to assume anything when handling this objection.

Not allowed due to company policy

As already discussed, there will be a reason why this decision was made, based on cost or previous experience. However, in many cases it is difficult to get a meeting with that decision-maker, and this must be your prime objective.

In cases where you cannot set up such a dialogue, I am assuming the conversation is taking place with someone responsible for actioning recruitment. It is important to establish their own view, in order to work out if the person you are talking to is a "friend or foe". You can elicit this information by simply asking: "How do you feel about that?" They may answer that they agree with the decision – in which case, you must address the reason that they do. Alternatively, if their objection is for a different reason to the company's position, you will need to address that first.

At this point you must tackle their objections, and in doing so, try and turn them into a friend who will help you reverse the corporate view. If they respond, "We would love to use recruitment agencies," then you have a potential ally whom you can work with going forward, without having to attempt to get them on-side.

Company has its own recruitment team

Consultants frequently react to this response with the question: "What do you do when they can't find you people?" It is a fair question but it can be counterproductive, especially if it puts the client on the defensive. It is important to understand why the decision was made to follow this strategy, so the advisable response is, "That's interesting, what is the recruitment process?" or putting a similar question.

It is more important than usual to listen now, as the tone of the response is crucial. We are assuming at this point that we are not talking to a member of the recruitment team, thus the tone will give you a clue as to whether the individual you are talking to thinks this is a good idea or not. Most organisations today measure their cost per hire (CPH). On occasion their CPH may be higher than the fee you would charge for the service, so this can be a huge opportunity to try and position your offering alongside their process.

If you can lead the discussion towards understanding what the component parts of their CPH are, you have invaluable information to find a way to dovetail what you offer with the in-house recruitment team. By understanding the process the client follows, you can explore individual stages of the process, as there is likely to be an element that could be improved. In order to exploit this opportunity, you are likely to need to be creative with your approach and normal service offering, to establish a revenue-generating opportunity with the client.

Example

You are following the process above, and you manage to establish that attracting candidates is an area for the client where you can add value. You must probe this further at this point. You have created a window of opportunity by understanding how they attract candidates. It is highly likely that there will be areas of generating candidates proactively that they are unaware of, but that you are. It is also likely that you have access to technology that helps handle candidate applications.

Discussing these options as a possible service that you could offer demonstrates your expertise and that the resultant cost savings would benefit them by reducing CPH.

Bad experience in the past

The first reaction – which is essential – is to apologise and empathise. However, you should ensure that your apology isn't too broad, suggesting that you accept responsibility at this stage; rather, a statement such as "I'm sorry to hear that" is appropriate. Never assume that it was or was not your own company involved until you establish the facts. Let's assume that the negative experience the client describes was with a competitor of yours. If so, establish what happened and apologise for the negative impact that it had, before explaining the controls in place at your company that ensure this could not happen.

Here, your approach is all about why your company would behave differently. If the experience in question relates to your own organisation, you must apologise sincerely, refocusing the emphasis on your own personal service standards. Try to avoid being negative about a colleague or former colleague who was involved at the time; instead, move your response towards how you would handle the situation, while stressing your values and the service levels that *you* deliver. To emphasise this, you must use the word "I" as frequently as possible, as your only hope of success is to personalise the situation, shifting the client's attention from the company to yourself.

No current recruitment requirements

Not every organisation will have a current requirement to recruit at the time that you are engaging with them. If this is the case, avoid falling into the trap of showing any disappointment, or allowing your energy to drop through your behaviour. Try and understand the volumes that are normally recruited and the frequency; also try to establish the client's recruitment history and future requirements, if there are any.

The key to positioning yourself well for the future is ascertaining the client's recruitment process, with the aim of gaining interest or commitment to engage you later. Follow this technique only if you are convinced it is the truth, and not a smokescreen for another objection.

Lack of understanding of the available services

Many clients will not understand the services that you offer, and so their perception potentially creates an objection that is not really there. In this situation it is important to revisit the potential requirements of the organisation, and marry the relevant features of your service that would benefit them. This is not as overcomplicated as you might think. For example, it could be that the organisation you are talking to only perceives your agency to supply temporary rather than permanent staff. As ever, never presume anything – ask the obvious question!

Viewing objections as a buying signal

Overall, most objection handling is about the strength of your ability to question, empathise and listen, which gives you the best opportunity of achieving a satisfactory outcome. As outlined previously, it's important to resist the temptation to counter before establishing the real objection and not to assume anything.

Finally, don't forget to approach this client interaction with the mentality that you will not be successful unless you overcome objections, and that their existence in the conversation is undoubtedly a buying signal. If you can change your mindset, you will experience a marked improvement in your success rate at overcoming objections. The natural reaction to objection is a lowering of energy and negative response. So, next time you face an objection, train your mind to think: "Great, this is an opportunity to forge a profitable relationship!"

Try it – it works!

4
The Candidate Interview

Interviewing a candidate effectively is one of the most important aspects of the recruitment consultant's role. It is an opportunity to assess their capability, understand their needs and attempt to see the situation through *their* own eyes. This is the time to build an understanding of, and rapport with, your candidate, so that you do not encounter misunderstandings later in the relationship that could impact on the organisation to which you introduce them. It is also an opportunity to glean the real motivation for their application, so that neither of you end up wasting time.

Seeing the situation through the candidate's eyes means that it is important to question rather than presume, because we naturally default to our own way of thinking.

Case study: Handling candidates

Let me take you back to the first ever vacancy I tried to fill, as a trainee consultant in the North of England. A vacancy was registered for a family engineering company, for someone to run the office and handle the accounts transactions. Ideally, the role would suit an experienced bookkeeper or office manager. The company was linked to an organisation in London, which in turn was linked to an organisation in America, but that was irrelevant to the role or – as I was to learn – to the candidate.

I duly submitted six candidates for the post, four of whom were selected for interview, and after discussion I persuaded the client to add another to make it five. It was then time to contact the candidates to arrange the interviews. During the initial conversation with the candidates to get permission to forward their details, I promised full specifications of the role if the submissions were successful, as I was pressed for time in competition with other agencies.

Seeing this job role through my eyes, it was an interesting one without many facets that would motivate me, so subconsciously I described it in a way that would be more appealing – as my naive belief was that everyone would want the same.

When I described the role to the five interviewees, the company was transformed into a "forward-thinking, rapidly-expanding, dynamic family company with exciting links to London and America". The role would offer promotion, challenge, probable UK travel and even possible travel to the United States! My enthusiasm and passion ensured that all the candidates agreed to attend the interview.

However, the outcome was that only one did attend – the reason being that they were scared off by my description of the role when really all they wanted was a pay rise, a good environment to work in, and an easier commute.

This is a prime example of poor candidate management through lack of understanding, rather than seeing the role through the candidate's eyes.

The seven steps

The candidate interview should follow the same journey as the sales call and client meeting.

1. Open

Explain the context of the meeting and what you want to achieve from the time spent together. Discuss the agenda, ask for honest responses and get an overview of the candidate's experience to enable you to find the most suitable role for them. In return you will provide feedback on their interview technique and a realistic appraisal of their aspirations being met: making your contract.

2. Question

Ask them to talk through their experience or CV to date. It is important to understand the reasons that the candidate has made their career decisions or changes this far. Also important is exploration and understanding of any gaps in their CV. The best way to ensure that you achieve this, and to ensure a natural flow for the discussion is, to start in the past or early stages of their work history, and work forward to the current time.

3. Listen

It is important to show interest in what the candidate has to discuss. Listening is not just keeping quiet while they talk – it is about hearing what they say. Often, trainees and experienced recruitment consultants are so focused on the goal they have for the meeting that they miss some key signals. Listening not only requires focus and effort, it also means paying attention to words, tone, language and voice. Moreover, it is important to notice the candidate's body language, and to hear what is not said.

It is easy to become distracted after a sentence or two because we are already thinking about *our* response. Control your body language: try not to demonstrate waning interest by lack of eye contact or incorrect posture. The message that this sends to the candidate is to stop talking, and may even upset them.

4. Clarify

In order to fully understand the candidate's experiences and achievements, make sure that you probe deeper where required, and ask for evidence of their accomplishments or more detail where insufficient information is naturally provided, in order to make an informed discussion about their ability and suitability. Again, do not presume anything. It is also time to establish the locations they will consider and salary required, although ideally you should note this rather than challenging expectations at this point.

5. Sell

Now is your opportunity to discuss current suitable vacancies with your candidate. If there are facets of the roles that the candidate has concerns about, this is the time to discuss and overcome those reservations. It is also your chance to widen the candidate's requirements, whether this be location, salary or type of role, because the less specific the requirement, the better the chance that you can help them.

6. Handle objections

The next action in this process is to challenge the candidate on how they would react to different scenarios. To illustrate this, let's assume a candidate has come to us. Currently, they are in a permanent role, and their main motivation for changing employer is for an increase in salary. They are underpaid, but they are happy with other aspects of their current organisation.

This candidate is a prime contender to be counter-offered by their current employer, if they give notice that they are leaving. There are two reasons why you need to discuss this possible scenario while interviewing the candidate: first, to gauge their reaction to the question; and second, to discuss the positives and negatives of changing their mind and staying put.

7. Close

The closing of the candidate interview is an opportunity to reconfirm your understanding and agree a mutually beneficial action plan. Honesty is key, as it is important to set realistic yet positive expectations of finding the desired role. It is also important to agree realistic and achievable levels of communication for your future relationship with them. Too little contact with a strong candidate and you run the risk of not finding them a role, while unnecessary communication with any candidate becomes a time thief.

5
Conclusion

The "magic circle" of recruitment

So far in this book we have discussed the client meeting, the business development call, handling objections and the candidate interview. You will have noticed that the structure of the telephone call, face-to-face meeting and candidate interview are very similar. In my opinion, all the other activities undertaken can be conducted in the same way. If you study the diagram below, and apply it in every situation, you will find a simple way of achieving success. It also relates to bids and tenders, although whereas the process takes about seven minutes or so on a good sales call, it would be drawn out over weeks, months or occasionally even years when applied to a tender.

The main advice is to follow the process, but to ensure that you do not progress to the next stage of the circle until you are happy that you have completed the previous one. If after handling objections you are unable to close, then loop back to questioning and revisit the stages one by one.

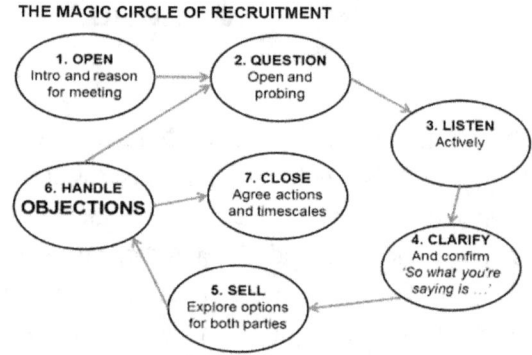

A final message

If there is one message that I would like anyone reading this book to take away, it's that the fundamentals have not changed, but everything else has. This statement was the penultimate sentence of the introduction, and is the first of the conclusion for good reason. The most fundamental tip to becoming a successful recruitment consultant is to follow the "magic circle" in all your interactions. By doing this, you can ensure you have all the information to find the right candidate for your client, and the right job for your candidate.

In my opinion, technology has revolutionised

the recruitment industry, but human interaction will always remain a fundamental part of the process. Combining these two areas will enhance your reputation and hone your expertise. The candidates you successfully place in suitable roles are highly likely to become clients of the future, so make sure you look after them. Never forget that every candidate you interact with is looking for a new role of some description. The majority of them will not achieve that goal through you, so make sure that you offer career guidance and support while setting realistic expectations with those you cannot help. Try not to forget how important career choices were for you, so you don't lose touch with the importance of this process to the individual you are trying to help.

A career in recruitment is unique: in the early years, the learning curve is steep and continuous, and no two individuals have their "lightbulb moment" at the same time, so don't panic if others seem to understand it more quickly than you. I guarantee that in your first year you are highly likely to have "What am I doing here?" and "I can't do this!" moments. I also predict that this will happen again and again in a lengthy career.

The best advice I can offer you is to focus and push yourself as hard as you can, because if recruitment is indeed right for you, by walking away you will be turning your back on one of the most challenging, varied and rewarding careers you can imagine. The highs are very high and the lows can be very low. But above all, don't forget: the customer is always right – even when they are wrong!

www.ingramcontent.com/pod-product-compliance
Lightning Source LLC
Chambersburg PA
CBHW071110240526
45469CB00006BD/2424